AMNESIA OF THE MOVEMENT OF CLOUDS

& OF RED AND BLACK VERSE

Originally published as *Amnesia del movimento delle nuvole* © 2003 by La Vita Felice, Milan and *Del rosso e del nero verso* © 2007 by Il Faggio, Milan.
Translation © 2014 by Carla Billitteri.

ISBN: 978-1-933959-42-9

Cover art: Thomas Flechtner. "Walk Nr. 1" from *Snow*, 2002. C-print mounted on aluminum.
75 ³⁄4 x 86 ¹⁄2 inches. Courtesy of the artist and Lars Müller Publishers
Author photo: Maurizio Orlando
Design & typesetting by HR Hegnauer | hrhegnauer.com
Text typeset in Spectrum.

Litmus Press is a program of Ether Sea Projects, Inc., a 501(c)(3) non-profit literature and arts organization. Dedicated to supporting innovative, cross-genre writing, the press publishes the work of translators, poets, and other writers, and organizes public events in their support. We encourage interaction between poets and visual artists by featuring contemporary artworks on the covers of our full-length books and in the pages of *Aufgabe*, our annual literary journal. By actualizing the potential linguistic, cultural, and political benefits of international literary exchange, we aim to ensure that our poetic communities remain open-minded and vital.

Litmus Press publications are made possible by the New York State Council on the Arts with the support of Governor Andrew Cuomo and the New York State Legislature. Additional support for Litmus Press comes from the Leslie Scalapino – O Books Fund, individual members and donors. All contributions are fully tax-deductible.

State of the Arts

NYSCA

Library of Congress Cataloging-in-Publication Data
Attanasio, Maria, 1943-
  Amnesia of the movement of clouds ; and, Of red and black verse / by Maria Attanasio ; translated by Carla Billitteri.
    pages cm
  Poems in Italian and English translation.
  First work originally published: Amnesia del movimento delle nuvole. Milano : La Vita Felice, 2003.
  Second work originally published: Del rosso e del nero verso. Milano : Il Faggio, 2007.
  ISBN 978-1-933959-42-9
  1. Attanasio, Maria, 1943---Translations into English. I. Billitteri, Carla, translator. II. Attanasio, Maria, 1943- Poems. Selections. III. Attanasio, Maria, 1943- Poems. Selections. English. IV. Title: Amnesia of the Movements of Clouds. V. Title: Of Red and Black Verse.
  PQ4861.T775A2 2013
  851'.914--dc23
                    2012043568

Litmus Press
925 Bergen Street; Suite 405
Brooklyn, New York 11238
litmuspress.org

Distributed by Small Press Distribution
1341 Seventh Street
Berkeley, California 94710
spdbooks.org

Maria Attanasio

TRANSLATED BY *Carla Billitteri*

AMNESIA OF THE MOVEMENT OF CLOUDS

& OF RED AND BLACK VERSE

AMNESIA OF THE
MOVEMENT OF CLOUDS

OF RED AND BLACK VERSE

POETRY, DUST, POLITICS

Born in 1943 in Caltagirone, where she lives today, Maria Attanasio is the author of seven books of poetry, four of historical fiction (three novels and a collection of short stories), two of utopian fiction, and two of literary and social criticism, with a number of other texts in various genres yet to be collected. In her recent *Della Città di Argilla* (*Of the City of Clay*, 2012), Attanasio presents herself as a political writer, a writer for whom militancy is a necessity—who considers political struggles "the deepest breath of history," "the invisible wings of history's becoming." She also presents herself as a remnant of the post-WWII, non-totalitarian Marxism that believed in the utopia of "a more just and shared world." Dismayed and disoriented by contemporary historical conditions, she would rather have been a child of the future, born in "the fourth or fifth century of the third millennium, so as to know how this history of wars and migrations, savage economic liberalism and starving populations, ended." Tellingly, she would still have the same family and town of origin in that future, for the fact of "belonging to the circumscribed spatiality" of Caltagirone, "pulsing with history, with stories, is at the origin," she writes, "of all my work... the metaphors of my poetry ...the microstories of my fiction."[1]

Caltagirone is one of the oldest towns in the southeast of Sicily; its beginning can be traced back to Neolithic times. A thriving center for ceramics production since the eighth century

BC, famous for its polychromatic majolica, Caltagirone was destroyed in 1693 by an earthquake and immediately rebuilt in the late Baroque style that is unique to this sector of Sicily. Today, Caltagirone is recognized by UNESCO as a world heritage site. A stronghold of agrarian aristocracy linked by way of family bonds to church hierarchy, Caltagirone maintained an extreme contrast of wealth and poverty far longer than anywhere else in Sicily. Until the late 1950s, the city kept a recognizably feudal profile of class differences: immediately below the aristocracy and the high ranks of catholic clergy stood the "*notabili*," a small number of upper- middle-class lawyers, bankers, and doctors whose services were linked to the aristocracy; below these toiled a large mass of working poor, some educated (teachers, clerks, shopkeepers, and artisans) some illiterate (servants, peasants, shepards), all living at or below the poverty line. Attanasio, her father a clerk, her mother a seamstress, grew up in this poverty, living with her brother and parents in a single *rez-de-chaussee* room with two small alcoves for toilet and stove. By saving ferociously, the family managed to send Maria to a Catholic school on the other side of town. She became aware of class differences early on there, when she was invited to the home of a classmate and discovered "the white and resplendent forms" of ceramic bathroom fixtures.[2] Up until that day, she had never known that clay—the basis of the city's wealth and industry—could be transformed into a beautiful, gleaming material. Her family had only a communal tub for washing made of yellow clay. Such clay, as Attanasio writes in her autobiography, dominated her family life: other familiar possessions included clay pots and dishes, and clay tiles covering the floor of the room they shared. Attanasio went on in the early 1960s to study philosophy at the University of Catania, where she became politically active, first as a representative in the city government for the Communist Party, later as an intellectual affiliated with the feminist movement to the left of the party.[3] She taught philosophy in high schools until the early 1990s, when she retired from teaching to dedicate herself to writing.

Attanasio began writing poetry in the late 1960s. As she mentioned in a recent conversation, she initially felt that writing was a betrayal of her militancy, but through her friendship with the poet Milo de Angelis she found "justification for a poetic consciousness." Her first collection, *Interni* (*Interiors*), was published in 1979 by Giovanni Raboni in *Quaderni della Fenice*, a prestigious book series gathering emerging poets writing in the tradition of Eugenio Montale. Attanasio's work appeared there next to Valerio Magrelli, who was also being published for the first time. Raboni termed Attanasio a poet of "ironic self-control," and irony is indeed a crucial trope in Attanasio's poetics. Hers is the irony of a postmodern Voltaire, irony as a form of philosophical inquiry attuned to conditions of uncertainty, of epistemic opacity, of not-knowing. Attanasio ascribes these conditions to the discontinuity between experiences and our cognition of them. This discontinuity manifests itself in the workings of memory, which, for Attanasio, is the principal mode of cognition. Remembering one's experience means becoming conscious of it, arriving at a narrativization of that experience. Attanasio presents memory as a site of division and uncertainty, for what we return to in it is only a partial representation of the past, an understanding disfigured by loss, brimming with void. With regard to history and society, memory is also brimming with violence. What memory can give is a sense of "the emptiness of the distance taken" between the immediate facts of experience and our understanding of them, but the arrival at such an understanding does not bring resolution, for the understanding that comes from recollection comes too late to have an impact on experience, comes too late to produce change.[4]

Attanasio directs her inquiry to sites of sorrow, places where the path to memory is obstructed and recollections are available only episodically, as fragments of meaning exposed to the corrosive cognition of loss. She describes the interior time of trauma, of receding visitations to domestic spaces that have long been abandoned or have become uninhabitable. Alienation accompanies these memories, for we cannot fully recover the meaning of our experiences, or, worse, cannot fully recognize it. The recollection of collectively experienced events can be equally traumatic, even when the experience comes at second hand (for the self of Attanasio's poems is always at a safe remove, enclosed in middle-class interiors), in news reports and television images: the devastation of wars, poverty, forced migration, human trafficking, child labor—these too are recollected in Attanasio's poetry in episodic flashes. In juxtaposing individually and collectively experienced events, direct and second-hand experiences, Attanasio retains a sense of proportion, and, indeed, recognizes a difference between the obstructed memory of personal loss and the ethical lethargy that sets historical losses at a safe remove. Her poems create a tension between the singularity of our own experience and the generality of history, often arriving at a precise rendering of the political paralysis created by the gap between public and private. Set in the perspective of global events, the traumas punctuating the private sphere do not lose for the reader the value of their epistemic opacity, but are weakened in their pathos: they become the matter of bourgeois discomfort. Thus, Attanasio's irony eventually turns her inquiry upon itself, exposing her own experience as permeated by false ideology, to employ a Marxist terminology. Irony, we could say, arrives at its highest affirmation in its own undoing. This kind of undoing is what Attanasio has described as "vertical writing," a call or injunction to deepen understanding. Verticality here does not elevate, it excavates; it does not accrue, it deconstructs. Together with irony, vertical writing is a poetics characterized by intellectually rigorous inquiry into the private and public dimensions of memory and their relation to unremembered experience.

In *Amnesia of the Movements of Clouds* (2003), the rigor of Attanasio's inquiry grapples with the cyborg dimensions of selfhood, in which thought, emotion, and memory are mediated by technology, beginning with the technology used to write the poem, the computer. Her poetry confronts and tries to appropriate, through a dialectic of recognition and misrecognition, the seemingly biomorphic manifestation of the technological apparatus, a manifestation Attanasio sets against the desolate political void of the new century—what she terms "the great amnesia," ascribed without nostalgia to "the god of ... indifference." While in *Amnesia* Attanasio's juxtaposition of individual and collective is played out in the relationship of body and machine, mind and apparatus, *Of Red and Black Verse* (2007) emphasizes the relation between personal memory and global awareness. As the matter of personal memories becomes more significant in this shorter collection, the social vision recedes, yet when it appears is more precise, even arresting, as, for instance, in the poem "Falluja." Attanasio sharpens the contrast between the stagnant, stolid indifference of daily living and the global suffering it tries to ignore. Indifference here becomes unapologetic callousness, as in the poem "(letter for a dead lover)." In his preface to the Italian edition of *Amnesia*, Giancarlo Majorino praises Attanasio for her courageous journey through the negative dimension of being. This journey continues in *Of Red and Black Verse*, a collection permeated by a deeper note of historical pessimism. I should note, however, that even when touching more personal registers, as in *Of Red and Black Verse*, Attanasio's journey through the negative is a political choice, and an aspect of her radical philosophy. On a few sporadic occasions, this negativity appears to be tempered, as for instance in "The Time to Come" (in *Amnesia*), where "a proletarian day announces itself" as a "cold breath on the nape of the neck / in the turn of an indifferent matter," a "swell of the tide" that "distantly resurges" on the other side of the hemisphere. This attenuated hope seems to echo what Ernst Bloch called "anticipatory consciousness," a diminished but not altogether extinguished belief in the possibility of change. Attanasio has frequently cited Bloch in her critical writing, and affirmed that in her poetry she seeks a vision of social justice, however remote and slow this swell of the tide appears to be.

In presenting the poetics of Maria Attanasio, I find myself struggling with the problem of her literary affiliations. Attanasio has always been careful to keep herself disaffiliated from specific poetic groups or poetic schools, and she has recently affirmed in an interview that disaffiliation is central to her politics of resistance.[5] In other interviews, however, she has expressed her love for the twentieth-century innovators of Italian poetry (Umberto Saba, Eugenio Montale, Amelia Rosselli, the last of these a dear friend), and indicated her admiration for the modernist expatriates Constantine Cavafy and Paul Celan as well as the Expressionists Georg Trakl and Gottfried Benn and the Surrealists Louis Aragon and Paul Éluard. Influences are forms of elective affinity, not institutional or social affiliations, and in what follows I will operate in accordance with this thinking, identifying a few of the important affinities Attanasio's work has with that of other twentieth-century Italian poets.

Stylistically, Attanasio belongs to the tradition of poets who make elegant use of varieties of regional Italian to underscore the social and cultural situatedness of their writing but also in a gesture of polemical distancing from the elevated language of poetry practiced by the hermetic tradition. Writers of regional Italian strive to maintain the syntax and the syntactical rhythms of the local dialect but do not employ dialect per se. Locality is affirmed and made active in a manner suggestive of Dante's invitation to write in a synthesized vernacular, a language particular enough to make evident the imprint of one's origins, but common enough so as to be understood by an audience extended beyond the local. Attanasio's emphasis on situatedness places her in conversation with the realist poets of "the Lombard line," a term originally coined by the critic and philosopher Luciano Anceschi in 1952 to describe a small group of poets whose "sober moral realism" he saw in opposition to the hermetic lineage of Salvatore Quasimodo and Giuseppe Ungaretti.[6] Drawing on T.S. Eliot's objective correlative and elaborating on the ideas of Edmund Husserl and Maurice Merleau-Ponty, Anceschi wrote that the poets of the Lombard line stay "*in re*," in things: inside the thinghood of living, permeable to all things. Their poetry is akin to phenomenological observation. It registers the continuous transformation of the subject as it lives in material relation to the world. Poets of the hermetic tradition, by contrast, stand "*ante rem*," before and outside things. Their stance presumes the priority and immutability of the subject, whose disposition is not changed by the interaction with—and is not permeable by—its materials. The realism of the Lombard line as defined by Anceschi rests in its attentiveness to the decentering of the self produced by living and inter-living with things. These are foundational premises for Attanasio's work, although her pronounced politics—not to mention her region, class, and gender—mark her distance from the contemporary successors of the Lombard line.

Also foundational is Attanasio's disposition toward a mode of poetic discourse brought forward by the experimental group of "I Novissimi" at the cusp of the 1960s and defined by Eugenio

Montale as "inclusive poetry." In Montale's words, inclusive poetry takes account of "the immense factory of technical progress," all the while communicating the discomforting consciousness that this factory is taking over and transforming our lives, that "the world is a serpent shedding its skin" and that "each one of us is the witness and the victim of this obscure mutation."[7] I Novissimi's engagement with a contemporary life threatening in its promise of continuous radical change was in theory all encompassing but in actual practice only touched the private sphere, the experiences of the individual.[8] For Attanasio, inclusiveness is both private and public, individual and collective, conceived from within a Marxist perspective. Inclusiveness makes manifest her situation as an engaged intellectual taking a stand with the working classes and the marginalized. Although she has always rejected ideological writing and has spoken in favor of a poetics of linguistic research (which, in Italy, has long been associated with elitism and conservative political positions), Attanasio does see poetry as a linguistic labor demanding to be understood like other forms of labor in a global and collective perspective. She shares with Montale and I Novissimi a suspicion of technology, but the politics of her suspicion are entirely different.

In conjunction with Attanasio's emphasis on a stylistically and intellectually situated discourse, those premises she shares with the *in re* poetics of the Lombard line and I Novissimi's inclusive poetry thicken her language. She calls this language "lingua lippusa," a Sicilian phrase that literally means "moss tongue."[9] This image conveys the sense of a poetic language that, like moss, is adhesively soft, holding its ground tenaciously while offering up a slippery surface: sticky, gluey, viscous. The mossiness of Attanasio's language—its holding fast to history while yielding, resisting, unbalancing, and tripping up in the present—exemplifies a postcolonial signifying practice deep in meaning for those accustomed to its ways, confounding to outsiders, keeping faith with history while turning against those who imposed it. The history of Sicily, an island at the crossroads of Europe and Africa, offers a rich ground for such a practice. Sicily was successively occupied by the Phoenicians, Greeks, Romans, Vandals, Byzantines, Arabs, Normans, Catalans, and Bourbons. Its population bears the traces of all these occupations and is diverse to this day in its blend of cultures and ethnicities. The diversity of Sicilian history is also reflected in the island's many dialects. Attanasio tries to honor this rich legacy. Her poetic research, she has remarked, is born out of "an imagination-producing interaction" of the spoken language and historical memory. It is a transcultural poetry operating simultaneously on several levels. The stratified materiality of sound, the syntax and rhythms of speech, produce a texture of recognition and negotiate with more ease than others. At the same time, this poetry remains meaningful outside the regional context, for Attanasio's linguistic transculturation is used in a manner that does not obstruct legibility, even when she uses terms from Sicilian dialect, though the approach to this work and the affect it arouses will necessarily be different for different audiences. This openness to different possibilities of reading is in keeping with Attanasio's belief that the self is always in permeable relation to others. Unfortunately, that aspect of her language cannot be transmitted in translation. What a translation can convey is the historical situation of Sicily today, which is, in fact, the situation of the whole world today: a crossroad of cultures under occupation. In some places, the occupation is military; in others, technological and economic. In some places, the landscape is traversed by armies and refugees; in others, the traversal occurs onscreen.

Attanasio's treatment of refugees, particularly prominent in *Amnesia*, deserves special attention here, for this condition of radical social marginalization is seldom if ever taken up in Italian poetry. In flight from political and economic hardship, from areas afflicted by famine, draught, war, and ethnic conflict, the refugees come on makeshift boats, often hundreds at a time, arriving on the coast of Sicily and on the shores of the islands off the south of Sicily, Linosa and Lampedusa. Many of them die during their journey (the crossing of the ocean takes many days in overcrowded boats with no food or water) or are discovered by the coast guard and forced to return to their departure points. Those who land are kept confined in open-air prison camps built in desolate rural areas and after a fixed period of time released with temporary papers that allow them to find work in the countries belonging to the European Union. Although the civic and humanitarian outrage is high when news of shipwrecks and deaths reach the public, such outrage is quick to subside. Public opinion is indifferent to the fate of refugees, if not unfavorably disposed toward non-European immigrants. There are few and impermanent economic measures in place for their support, and, as the rise of right-wing parties and neo-Nazi groups and racist attacks in Spain, France, Italy, Germany, Sweden, Norway, and Denmark can testify, refugees face organized violence, often approved at the government level. The term "clandestines" is commonly used to name these refugees in the press and public discourse, and this is the word that appears in Attanasio's poetry; I have adopted it here for this translation. The term perfectly captures the common belief in Europe that refugees belong out of sight, hence their removal to camps in the countryside. The clandestines exist, as it were, in the crypt of European consciousness.

Attanasio provides quick, unsentimental snapshots of the racist brutality awaiting refugees and casts a harsh glance at the ideology of sameness sustaining the widespread social indifference to—if not embrace of—such brutality. Her poetry is intended as an interruption of silence and indifference. At the same time, her critical response to the ideology of sameness links the politics of her work to her philosophical inquiry, as difference and alterity are what call the self to account and so make an issue of subjectivity as such. Attanasio treats subjectivity as a site of continuously modified and modifying relations. In her analysis, the subject exists in precarious balance between inward and outward. There is, in her poems, a centripetal accumulation of memories and sense perceptions sustained in dynamic tension with a centrifugal dispersion caused by contingency, interaction, and experience. The more precarious the balance and dynamic the tension, the more problematic an issue subjectivity becomes. In such crises, the self is made progressively foreign to its own certainties, exposed to the randomness of existence. Hers is a multiperspectival poetry agitated by epistemic dissatisfaction. In this Attanasio is close to Amelia Rosselli, whose attunement to the quotidian manifested itself in allegories of estrangement—*spaesamento* in Italian, literally the sense of being outside one's village (one's *paese*). The *spaesamento* of Attanasio is political and philosophical: the emergence of past events in her poems is not strictly confessional. Even at its most personal, her poetry records, in minimal increments as well as in the incremental curve of recurring scenes, motifs, and settings, a graph of collective experiences.

Attanasio's account of subjectivity is enlarged by the interest in objecthood she shares with the poets of the Lombard line. In both *Amnesia* and *Of Red and Black Verse* there is a productive relation between memory and the object-world. Self-recognition is not located in memory, but in objects, especially those of the domestic environment, which continually *provoke* memory. In many poems, the reconstruction of the disposition of daily possessions on night tables and writing desks delineates the field of cognition, defines the sense of a past. Dispersed in experiences, subjectivity is found outside itself. It is only fitting that *Amnesia* opens with an epigraph from E. M. Cioran: "life is the romance of matter." Even in its most elemental form, matter pervades Attanasio's work, from the clay of Caltagirone to the rot of leaves to the whirlpool of the ocean to the planetary dust of the Oort cloud. In many ways, the best account of Attanasio's poetry would be a list of this matter, or, better, its incorporation in an emblem such as one sees on the flag of every municipality in Italy. Inscribed in this emblem would be three words bound by their initial letter, "*Poesia, Polvere, Politica*": poetry, dust, politics, because, for Attanasio, dust (which is to say life) and politics (which is to say "justice") "are inseparable from poetry."[10] This emblem would also serve for the city of her memory, which her poetry reinhabits and her prose reconstructs—hence the title of her most autobiographical book, *Of the City of Clay*. Attanasio's poetry is formed with that clay fired in struggle—a language bound to life and justice. This is what she offers us in the historical moment we share with her.

A number of friends have marked the path of this project. To these I address my thoughts with love and gratitude: Concetta Cavallotto, who introduced me to the poetry in the summer of 1998 and put me in contact with Maria Attanasio; Jenniffer Scappettone and Giovanni Miraglia, whose gifts for multilingual translation I will never match. Jennifer prompted my first translations of *Amnesia* and then invited Maria to read her poetry in New York and Chicago; Giovanni has inspired and encouraged me with his wit and exquisite wisdom for forty years. Special thanks to Maria Attanasio, for being such a graceful and generous correspondent, and to Benjamin Friedlander, whose nurturing companionship, love of poetry and fine-grained intelligence made this and many other projects possible. A deep debt of gratitude goes to Tracy Grinnell, who envisioned, sponsored, and attended every aspect of this project with incomparable care.

— CARLA BILLITTERI

Bangor, Maine

June 2013

NOTES

1 *Della cittá di argilla* (Messina: Mesogea, 2012), 7.

2 *Della cittá di argilla*, 12.

3 It might be of interest to note here that Attanasio's second historical novel, *Di Concetta e le sue donne* (*Of Concetta and Her Women*, 1999) recovers the history of Concetta La Ferla, a member of the Italian Communist Party, born in Caltagirone in 1930, who founded the first constituency of communist women in the Party in the 1950s and organized one of the largest and most successful strikes of rural workers in the history of southern Italy. Notwithstanding her contributions, La Ferla could not rise through the male-dominated ranks and was eventually pushed out of the Party.

4 I borrow this phrase, "the emptiness of the distance taken" from Louis Althusser, *Philosophy and the Spontaneous Philosophy* (London: Verso 1990), 197.

5 "Una poeta e le sue personagge" ("A woman poet and her women characters"), interview with Gisella Modica for the Società Italiana delle Letterate," September 2012. http://www.societadelleletterate.it/2012/09/una-poeta-e-le-sue-personagge

6 Anceschi's original grouping included only six poets, born in the 1920s, sharing the same area of geographic provenance: Luciano Erba, Nello Ortese, Roberto Rebora, Nelo Risi, and Vittorio Sereni. This grouping was later expanded so as to include the work of poets of previous or subsequent generations belonging to regions other than Lombardy: Sergio Caproni, Franco Fortini, Pier-Paolo Pasolini, Maria Luisa Spaziani, Giovanni Raboni, and Milo De Angelis.

7 Eugenio Montale, "Poesia inclusiva" (1964), reprinted in *Il secondo mestiere. Arte, musica e società*, a cura di G. Zampa, Milano, Mondadori, 1996.

8   I speak here of I Novissimi at the beginning of the 1960s, and from Montale's perspective, which I find precise. As the 1960s went forward, the poets of the I Novissimi shared in the general politicization undergone by culture in that decade, but this in fact led to the fracturing of the group as group in 1969.

9   "Lippu" means "moss" in Sicilian; "lippusa" is the feminine adjectival form of the noun, "lippu." Figuratively, "lippusa" or "lippuso" (the masculine form of the adjective) characterize anything that tenaciously persists through time, something old if not ancient. These connotations point to Attanasio's persistent interest in the history of Sicilian language and in Sicilian history, an aspect of her poetics that can be best appreciated in her prose works.

10   "Una poeta e le sue personagge," interview with Gisella Modica.

AMNESIA DEL
MOVIMENTO DELLE NUVOLE

———————————

AMNESIA OF THE
MOVEMENT OF CLOUDS

POESIE D'AMORE IN TEMPO DI GUERRA

————————————

LOVE POEMS IN A TIME OF WAR

"La vita é il romanzo della materia"
E. M. CIORA N

"Life is the romance of matter"
E. M. CIORA N

I

Mentre il tempo accovacciato
sull'albero tende le orecchie
a un cielo d'invisibili laser
un brusio di impronte digitali
sulle maniglie delle porte la tua
nudità esposta a ogni attentato
il campo di luce si restringe tocca
lo zero senza morso di bacio oblio
di sigaretta regredendo in fissità.

II

Una frazione di non coincidenza,
tela di ragno, astro,
tra la mia vita e il tuo millennio
le buie armate della mezzanotte
sfaldano la città e le sue luci
lo stacco della mente
il taglio netto tra la pace e la guerra
il profilo della città sull'altura
infinitamente nero.

I

As time crouched
in the tree turns ears
to a sky of invisible lasers
a murmur of digital prints
on the doorknobs your
nudity exposed to every attack
the field of light shrinks touches
the zero without kiss's bite oblivion
of the cigarette regressing in fixity.

II

A fraction of noncoincidence,
spider web, star,
between my life and your millennium
dark armies of midnight
cleave the city and its lights
the split of the mind
the clean cut between war and peace
the profile of the city on high ground
infinitely black.

III

Quale chimica oggi quale
lenzuolo stendere nella stanza
che il vento mise a ferro e fuoco
Giovanni d'amnesia, osare d'aghi,
aspettando la fine dell'embargo
la tregua
della tua mano sul mio sesso.

IV

Senza difesa di salvagente mentre
oltrepassi la soglia al richiamo di palestre
e bancarelle dalla città sull'altura,
risalendo il sesso l'ombelico
trattenerti nella luce a spirale della stanza
con l'umido della saliva la scrittura latente
della lingua che rimuove l'anellide maligno
nel vestibolo incatena la vertigine—fuori
la gazza ruba ciliege becca viscere.

III

What chemistry today what
linen spread in the room
that wind put to iron and fire
Giovanni of amnesia, daring of needles,
waiting the end of the embargo
the truce
of your hand on my sex.

IV

Without defense of life-preserver while
you cross the threshold recalled by gyms
and street-stalls from the city on high ground,
reclimbing sex the navel
holding you back in the coiled light of the room
with dampness of saliva the latent writing
of the tongue that removes the malignant anellid
in the vestibule chains the vertigo—outside
the magpie steals cherries pecks viscera.

V

Un fulmine una grande cascata
una corrente di tempo futuro
nella camera di sublimazione
lo zolfo bagnato la bic esaurita
dismesso
l'amore che fu zolfanello poesia.

VI

Un piede avanti poi l'altro
l'abisso del non senso il vuoto
di memoria tra passo e passo
l'invalicabile presenza di Zenone
nel cerchio infinito dell'abbraccio
era certezza reversibile, quanto,
sapienza di milioni anni luce
alle spalle il padre monatto scavava
buche risaliva a bocca spalancata.

V

A flash of lightning a great cascade
a current of future time
in sublimation's room
the sulphur wet the bic inkless
dimissed
the love that was a match a poem.

VI

One foot forward then the other
the abyss of no sense the void
of memory between step and step
insurmountable presence of Zeno
in the infinite circle of embrace
it was reversible certainty, quantum,
wisdom of millions of light years
behind it the father monatto dug
ditches climbed out with gaping mouth.

VII

Parlare della morte poi scopare
o litigare a più non posso—lei
s'appiattiva nell'angolo: per te
in forma di ragno per me
di scarafaggio, cieca, paralizzata,
morta la morte—le guglie tremavano
le maniglie delle porte si aprivano
da sole la bellezza era vicina di tavolo
e compagna di letto il passo barocco
acuminato nell'anima che mi hai dato.

VIII

Tagli di luce obliqua nella stanza
l'attimo dell'amore dissipato
in fondo a città regresse nel sonno
tribù erranti nella boscaglia all'alba
il sibilo di bombardieri in formazione
il canto strangolato del gallo.

VII

To talk about death and then to fuck
or fight as hard as we can—she
squashed herself in a corner: for you
in the shape of a spider for me
of a roach, blind, paralyzed,
dead death—steeples trembled
doorknobs opened
of themselves beauty was at next table
and a bed companion the baroque step
acute in the soul that you gave me.

VIII

Shafts of light oblique in the room
the moment of love wasted
at the bottom of cities regressed in sleep
errant tribes in the brush at dawn
the hiss of bombers in formation
the strangled crow of the rooster.

IX

Il libro aperto sul comodino gli occhiali
abbandonati sul letto la nudità,
la mattina, fra sigaretta e caffettiera,
murati con una pallottola di calce
—la casa ristrutturata—come se mai
fosse stata scrittura di cellule
luce dell'alfabeto.

X

L'assenza, adesso, l'immagine
soltanto immaginata—solo,
assetato, il fresco gorgogliare
sperso in una notte di siccità—
mentre dalla città che si risveglia
un brusio di luce mattinale
lo sorprende insonne alla finestra.
L'isola dall'orizzonte si stacca,
controcorrente si allontana.

IX

The book opened on the night table the eyeglasses
abandoned on the bed the nudity,
in the morning, between cigarette and coffeemaker,
walled in with a bullet of plaster
—the home restructured—as if there never
had been a writing of cells
light of the alphabet.

X

The absence, now, the image
only imagined—lonely,
thirsty, the cool gurgling
adrift in a night of drought—
while from the city that reawakens
a murmur of diurnal light
surprises him insomniac by the window.
The island unfastens itself from the horizon,
departs against the current.

XI

Con morso di bacio nella gola
tra sbarchi clandestini
bulldozer nelle spianate
asimmetrico moto d'onda che viene
nell'indistinto della traversata
dove l'amore sta precipitando
(una morte romantica, alla Kleist,
un testo senza ironia.)

XII

Gli oggetti in disuso nella stanza
ripetuta allo specchio della vita
in leggerezza di parola il mondo
evaporato in chiarità era
la sabbia della notte Africana
a risalire, su noi forse esistenti.

XI

With kiss's bite stuck in the throat
amid clandestine landings
bulldozers on flattened land
asymmetrical motion of wave that comes
in the indistinctness of the crossing
where love is crashing down
(a Romantic death, after Kleist,
a text without irony.)

XII

The objects in disuse in the room
repeated in the mirror of life
in light words the world
evaporated in clarity was
sand of African night
resurging, on us perhaps existant.

ROSA A FRAMMENTI

(in memoria di Rosy Castiglione)

ROSE IN FRAGMENTS

(in Memory of Rosy Castiglione)

Ne' il sole ne' la morte si possono guardare fisso
LA ROCHEFOUCAULT

———————————

Neither sun nor death can be stared at fixedly
LA ROCHEFOUCAULT

1 (SIGARETTA)

   Senza segni premonitori
   la sigaretta sviò dall'altra parte.
   A prendere fuoco furono i capelli
   —biondi, arruffati—
   bianco, appena qualche filo,
   occultato con cura crepitava.

2 (KAJAL)

   I nodi, al risveglio,
   le schricchiolanti connessioni
   a strapiombo nella notte—il respiro
   si fa pietrisco nello specchio: kajal
   che preme ai bordi punta al centro—
   gorgogliando nei nomi ogni mattina
   nel residuo di passi della madre.

1 (CIGARETTE)

Without premonitory signs
the cigarette turned the other way.
What caught fire was the hair
—blonde, tousled—
white, just a few strands,
hidden with care crackled.

2 (KAJAL)

The knots, upon awakening,
the creaking connections
a vertical drop in the night—the breath
turns into gravel in the mirror: kajal
that presses at the borders points to the center—
gurgling into names each morning
in the residue of mother's steps.

3 (BRACCIALETTO)
Il nucleo il gorgo il vento
di maestrale in cavo braccialetto
—si rigonfia scoppia—arriva
quatto quatto l'esperto
prende il coltello la lima infila l'ago.

4 (BANCARELLE)
Un brusio di mercati a pieno sole
forza la blindata opacità
della sghemba vigilia nello specchio
ricompone le sillabe del nome—i petali
le spine l'oro in letargo sul comodino—
il passo claudicante torna
vita opalina lampeggiante cavigliera.

3 (B R A C E L E T)
    The nucleus the whirlpool the wind

    of mistral in hollow bracelet

    —it swells explodes—arrives

    ever so quiet the expert

    takes the knife the file threads the needle.

4 (S T R E E T   S T A L L S)
    A murmur of markets in full sun

    breaks open the armored opacity

    of lopsided vigil in the mirror

    recomposes the syllables of the name—the petals

    the thorns the gold lethargic on the night table—

    the halting step returns

    opaline life blazing ankle brace.

5 (OGGETTI)

Si muovono si precipitano
addosso, gli infedeli,
con libri di preghiere e scimitarre
—tegole armadi specchi—
tracce d'antrace nei cassetti
senza residue di briciole il tagliere.

6 (ROSA A FRAMMENTI)

Il fard sul comò la morfina le sigarette
il suo profilo sghembo tra zinco e saldatrice
—il sibilo spegne
il rossofiamma divarica lo stretto—
rosa a frammenti
nella cieca spazialità di mare aperto.

5 (OBJECTS)

They move tumble down
against us, the infidels,
with prayers books and scimitars
—tiles cupboards mirrors—
tracks of anthrax in the drawers
without crumbs residue the cutting board.

6 (ROSE IN FRAGMENTS)

The blush on the dresser the morphine the cigarettes
her slanted profile between zinc and welder
—the hiss extinguishes
the redflame spreads open the strait—
rose in fragments
in the blind spatiality of the open sea.

7 (MAESTRALE)

    I roghi di mezza estate quando la vita

    geme la sua perdita in granelli di sabbia

    in spire di maestrale che oscurano

    i gigli le rose di maggio. Sbianca

    il volto abbronzato d'Agosto, gli acini

    i grappoli spersi dei tuoi vigneti, Settembre.

8 (SCHERMO)

    I titoli di coda—gli abiti

    gli oggetti le citazioni—

    disperso il nome degli attori

    la domestica scena

    si svuotò: un fu di righe rombi

    di liquide spirali in schermo nero.

7 (M I S T R A L)

> Midsummer bonfires when life
> moans its loss in grains of sand
> in spirals of mistral that obscure
> the lilies the roses of May. Pales
> the tanned face of August, the grapes
> the scattered clusters of your vineyards, September.

8 (S C R E E N)

> The credits—the dresses
> the objects the citations—
> displaced the name of the actors
> the domestic scene
> emptied itself: a past of lines rhombuses
> of liquid spirals on black screen.

(Rosa appartata, ombrosa, amò
i frutti di fuori stagione, la vita
disegnata nella mente—gli amanti
immaginati il segreto tintinnio
di braccialetti—non resa, consegna
al niente: in quell'inverno
d'oscuramento contro l'astuto invasore
fu spada lucente arcangelo Michele.)

(Rose withdrawn, morose, loved
fruits out of season, a life
drawn in the mind—imagined
lovers the secret jingle
of bracelets—unsurrendered, consigned
to nothingness: in that winter
of obfuscation against the cunning invader
was shining sword archangel Michael.)

DELLA FORZATA RIMA

OF FORCED RHYME

Per far consonare ciò che talvolta non è consonante;
forzare a dire, attraverso un ludico, sadico, gioco di suoni,
ciò che altrimenti——per mancanza di parole o per troppo
orrore——nella contemporaneità resta invisibile.
LOUIS SOLIANO

———————————

To consonate what is sometimes not consonant; to force
the saying, by way of a ludic, sadistic play of sounds,
of what otherwise——for lack of words or too much
horror——remains invisible in our times.
LOUIS SOLIANO

PRIMO MOVIMENTO:
DELLA MORTE BUTTANA

———————————

FIRST MOVEMENT:
OF DEATH BITCH

INCIPIT (UN NOME A CASO)

Lisa lisetta lisavetta
che giri il chiavistello della porta
—atro ostello nella stellata,
debordante ab imis, notte—
ora, ora impostora, atra sorte:
tic tac che spingi alla morte.

COMPLEANNO

Giorno virtuale senza virtù né vizi
senza nebbie né sole meridiano
dies ille nullatenente giovedì
di files smagnetizzati di erbe spente
dal buio
lampeggiando spirate spire.

INCIPIT (A NAME BY CHANCE)

Lisa lisetta lisavetta

you who turns the bolt of the door

—dark hostel in the starred,

overflowing ab imis, night—

hour, impostor hour, bitter fate:

tick tock that pushes on toward death.

BIRTHDAY

Virtual day with no virtues or vices

with no fogs or meridian sun

dies ille destitute Thursday

of demagnetized files of spent grass

from the dark

flashing expired spires.

ALIMENTARISTA

Vi allevai con rigore di alimentarista
—l'origano, la menta, l'acqua
dei giardini di Machado—
ma il delirio vi assalì lo stesso, cellule,
nella casa senza orme e battenti
la mente alluciata l'intonaco sconnesso.

REPENTE

Repente, ahi dolore della mente,
come se niente fosse la notte
senza salvacondotti allupata.
La mano trema la casa vacilla.

NUTRITIONIST

I nursed you with a nutritionist's rigor
—oregano, mint, water
from the gardens of Machado—
but delirium attacked you all the same, cells
in the house with no prints or shutters
the mind blinded the plaster decrepit.

SUDDENLY

Suddenly, ah pain of the mind,
as if the night were nothing
without safe-conducts ravenous.
The hand trembles the house vacillates.

IL GRANDE ATTO

Il grande atto l'impatto
quotidiano—ostruzione a volte
rimozione—è vacua azione
(il topo risale lo stesso
a rosicchiare il terminale).

FUSIONE

Viola melenzana—suono a lutto
convessa manovella—orto
ben irrigato di paura: legata
stretta, bendata, la lancetta
nel punto di fusione.

THE GREAT ACT

The great act the impact
quotidian—obstruction sometimes
elimination—is empty action·
(the mouse reclimbs all the same
to gnaw the terminal).

FUSION

Eggplant purple—mourning sound
convex handle crank—garden
well watered with fear: bound
tightly, blindfold, needle
at the melting point.

MOVIMENTO DI TRASLAZIONE

Deviato dal sito
traslato
in nube silicica in neve polare
spolpato ossicino
tra acidi sali galleggiando
lieve.

LACCATA DI ROSSO

Poesia dagli occhi gonfi
che ti disfi in cartone bagnato
in minimali sequenze in bianco e nero,
di nuovo il galoppo nell'affollato
moussem, resisti al cieco fondale
balbetti un avido sì,
rifatta nuova, laccata di rosso.

MOVEMENT OF TRANSLATION

Diverted by the site
translated
in silica cloud in polar snow
bare little bone
among acid salts floating
softly.

VARNISHED IN RED

Poetry with puffy eyes
you come undone in wet carton
in minimal sequences in black and white,
again the gallop in the crowded
moussem, resist the blind backdrop
stammer an avid yes,
remade new, varnished in red.

LAMPO

Lampo di melograno

fiamma di malvasia

in una stanza globalizzata

rosso di poesia.

Il buio adesso, un attimo fa ero Maria.

DELETE

Delete distrattamente digitato

tutto fonde e non si arresta

—mia madre azzerata i libri spenti—

da una fessura mentale trabocca

in un giorno feriale l'onda anomala

di una bianca notte polare.

FLASH

Flash of pomegranate
flame of malvasia
in a globalized stanza
red of poesia
Darkness now, a moment ago I was Maria.

DELETE

Delete hit distractedly
melts everything and doesn't stop
—my mother zeroed out among spent books—
from a crack of the mind overflows
in a weekday the anomalous wave
of a white polar night.

DERAGLIATA RIMA

L'assonanza tra rima deragliata
rima nel brulicare di sotto
—treno fuori binario strappo
dell'armonia in impreviste contrade—
buio il cammino incerto il senso.

MORTE BUTTANA

Morte buttana onda d'invertebrati
vaso del mio pensiero in latitanza
dal buco del tuo sesso
rompe gli argini avanza nella pianura
l'occhio spento di dio.
Notte incandescente ossidiana.

DERAILED RHYME

The assonance in derailed rhyme
rhyme in the swarming underneath
—train off track strain
of harmony in unexpected quarters—
dark the path uncertain the sense.

DEATH BITCH

Death bitch wave of invertebrates
vessel of my thought in hiding
from the hole of your sex
splits the banks advances in the plane
the spent eye of god.
Night incandescent obsidian.

SECONDO MOVIMENTO:
DELLA RIMA IN ÌA

———————————

SECOND MOVEMENT:
OF IA RHYME

PASSATO (IN ERI)

Nuda, alla corda,

in un tribunale del milleseicento

tra gli incensieri della buona morte

—notte di stendardi e incappucciati

Steri d'inesauribile durata—

mai luce se non fiamma di rogo.

RITORNI

Un crepitare di roghi, un vociare,

la notte, gli scafisti—le prove inquinate

il paesaggio svuotato dagli spot—prosciolto

da ogni colpa il passo cadenzato risale

sull'altura si accampa dietro i vetri

si masturba. All'alba

idillio e colazione nel paesaggio ristrutturato.

PAST (YOU WERE)

    Naked, in rope,

    in a tribunal of the sixteenth century

    among the censers of good death

    —night of banners and hooded men

    Steri of inexhaustible duration—

    never light but blaze of stake.

RETURNS

    A crackling of bonfires, a shouting,

    the night, the smugglers—the proofs corrupted

    the landscape drained by spotlight—cleared

    of all blame the measured step walks back

    on the hill pitches camp behind glass

    masturbates. At dawn

    idyl and breakfast in the restructured landscape.

NOTIZIA DI CRONACA (11 GENNAIO '99)

Lama di sale che scopre la ferita

tra il primo caffè e la sigaretta

in un sottosuolo invernale

di cannucce schiacciate di cicche spente

la buia enclave

l'esecuzione, stanotte, a Bogotà.

FEZ (TAPPETI D'OCCASIONE)

Frusciare d'acque reflue di tinture

—la porpora l'oro il verde ramina—

tappeti d'occasione

tra le volte dell'affollata Medina

sure tessute a mano

tra nodo e nodo dita di bambini.

LOCAL NEWS (11 JANUARY 1999)

Blade of salt that exposes the wound

between first coffee and cigarette

in a wintry underground

of crushed thin reeds cigarette butts

the dark enclave

the execution, last night, in Bogotà.

FEZ (BARGAIN RUGS)

Swishing of waste water of dyes

—the purple the gold the copper green—

bargain rugs

under the vaults of the crowded Medina

surahs woven by hand

between knot and knot fingers of children.

NOTIZIA DI CRONACA (CON CRIPTOCITAZIONE)

30 cartoni per la traversata
ma Amed, il marocchino,
nulla attraversò—né ipermercati
né metropolitane—zavorra
di scafisti in onda di maestrale
respiro annegato.

NOTIZIA DI CRONACA (20 MARZO 2000)

Roma sottonotte di ultras—clandestini
cosparsi di benzina—combusti resti
tra i cartoni del sottopassaggio
quietamente
sbucciando piselli in cucina.

LOCAL NEWS (WITH CRYPTIC CITATION)

30 cigarette cartons for the crossing

but Amed, the Moroccan,

crossed nothing—no megastores

no subways—ballast

of smugglers in mistral wave

drowned breath.

LOCAL NEWS (20 MARCH 2000)

Rome undernight of ultras—clandestines

sprayed with gasoline—combusted remains

amid the cartons of the underpass

quietly

shelling peas in the kitchen.

LUDICA MENTE

Ludica mente

nell'amnetica luce satellitare

la terra

un giro di compasso pacificato

ai margini un'oscurata finisterre

di stralunati chirurghi

la strada di passi chiodati.

RIMA IN *ALE*

Il gorgo la labirintica spirale

in forma

di campo di sterminio di soluzione

finale—amnetico fondo

tra muraglie e lingue straniere

dove inizia la notte.

PLAYFUL MIND

Playful mind

in the amnesiac light of satellites

the earth

a pacified turn of the compass

at the margins an obscured finisterre

of dazed surgeons

the road of spiked footsteps.

AL RHYME

The whirlpool the labyrinthine spiral

in shape

of an extermination camp of final

solution—amnesiac ground

between ramparts and foreign tongues

where night begins.

SCRITTURA

Tra un brusio di migranti
a occidente con passo asiatico
con mani africane risale i bordi,
scrittura deragliata nel millennio
finestra che precipita nel bianco.

(FORZATA) RIMA IN *ÌA*

In una teca in un blocco di sale
costretta alla rima sciolta in liquide
vocali—il sistema operativo azzerato
l'utopia cancellata dagli hackers
durante il trasloco—storìa
di canto inverso di arti amputati
tra sibili di fax squilli di cellulari.

WRITING

In a murmur of westward
migrants with Asiatic step
with African hands reclimbs the confines,
writing derailed in the millennium
window that drops in the white.

(F O R C E D) *IA* R H Y M E

In a reliquary in a block of salt
forced to a rhyme dissolved in liquid
vowels—the operative system set to zero
the utopia erased by the hackers
during the move—historia
of inverse song of amputated limbs
among the hissing of faxes ringing of cellphones.

LIBERO MERCATO

Che altro

nella notte dei lunghi coltelli

se non un privato gioco di rime

per rimuovere l'immagine ostinata:

occhi polmoni arti riciclati al dettaglio

il resto in traboccanti discariche.

FREE MARKET

What else

in the night of long knives

but a private game of rhyme

to remove the obstinate image:

eyes lungs limbs recycled for retail

the rest in overflowing landfill.

IL DIO DEI GIORNI
UGUALI E DELLA INDIFFERENZA

———————

THE GOD OF INDISTINCT
DAYS AND INDIFFERENCE

BIVIO DEL SÌ E DEL NO

Bivio del sì e del no vita binaria
senza furore di complessità
tra i virus le sconnessioni del millennio
sorella d'ostinata permanenza
cliccando a vuoto nel liquido fondale
una nube passa distratta sul mondo
memoria volatile nella precipita notte.

PAROLE

Tra gorghi trombe d'aria in una pianura
di cingolati e militari a passo di essese
parole come guerra indifferenza armate
di bazooka contro i vetri antisfondamento
onda di giallo che più non separa
giorno e notte nella stanza che si fa deserto.

CROSSROAD OF YES AND NO

Crossroad of yes and no binary life

without fury complexity

among the viruses the disconnections of the millennium

sister of obstinate permanence

clicking in vain in the liquid backdrop

a cloud passes distracted over the earth

volatile memory in the precipitous night.

WORDS

Between whirlpools whirlwinds on a plain

of tanks and armies with goose steps

words as war indifference armed

with bazookas against bulletproof glass

yellow wave that no longer separates

day and night in the stanza that becomes desert.

INVARIANZA

Era bianco di luglio nella magnolia
ed è caos di foglie enzima ribelle
a ostruire l'uscita—vita volvit in favilla
in entropia di proteine—invarianza
davanti la porta di strelizie e uliveti
senza battiti né pulsazioni.

IL DIO DEI GIORNI UGUALI

Spente le luci sbarrate le porte
s'insinua nel letto tra di noi—il dio
dei giorni uguali e dell'indifferenza—
complice della cieca mezzanotte inverte
mappe e rotte il vento agita lamiere
la linea blu del mare si aggroviglia.

INVARIANCE

It was white of July in the magnolia
and is chaos of leaves rebellious enzyme
that obstructs the exit—vita volvit in favilla
in entropy of proteins—invariance
in front of the door of strelitzia and olive groves
without heartbeat or pulse.

THE GOD OF INDISTINCT DAYS

The lights turned off the doors locked
it slips in the bed between us—the god
of indistinct days and indifference—
accomplice of blind midnight inverting
maps and routes the wind agitates sheets of corrugated metal
the blue line of the sea becomes entangled.

AVVISO DI SFRATTO

Stamattina tutti i gerani cantavano ai balconi
le mosche cavalline le ostinate file di formiche
—luccicava la polvere negli angoli i libri
di vivide scritture: storie di mare
pulsanti archivi di poesia—e anche l'intonaco
il rumore dello sciacquone il fiato
che saliva leggero nel mondo stamattina
davanti al caffè e all'avviso di sfratto.

IL TEMPO CHE VERRÀ

Un giorno proletario si annuncia. Il tempo
che verrà respiro freddo sulla nuca
nel giro di una materia indifferente
alla oscurate procedure di uranio e di grafite
mentre dall'altra parte della mappa—in qualche
remota polinesia—è già chiaro il mattino
tra gli atolli. Un'onda di marea
sveglia i molluschi, lontanissima risale.

EVICTION NOTICE

    This morning the geranium sang from the balconies

    the horse-flies the obstinate lines of ants

    —the dust sparkled in the corners the books

    of vivid writing: stories of the sea

    pulsating archives of poetry—and even the plaster

    the noise of the toilet flush the breath

    that rose lightly in the world this morning

    with the coffee and the eviction notice.

THE TIME TO COME

    A proletarian day announces itself. The time

    to come cold breath on the nape of the neck

    in the turn of an indifferent matter

    to the concealed procedures of uranium and graphites

    while on the other side of the map—in some

    remote polynesia—the morning is already clear

    over the atolls. A swell of the tide

    awakens the mollusks, distantly resurges.

ESTERNO

Dispersa corsa per la marcita
la fungaia la dissennata campagna
l'autunno in rivoli in grumi raffermi.
In ostinato raschiare di cani alla porta.

LETARGO

Raccogliere le cose fare in fretta
prima che il letargo dilati la distanza
tra la mano e la porta
—la tana scavata con cura nella carta:
paglia provviste rami secchi—
accesa la lanterna
che nel secolo fu tempesta e fiamma.

EXTERIOR

Scattered run through the water meadow
the mushroom bed the senseless countryside
the autumn in rivulets in stale clumps.
In obstinate scraping of dogs at the doorstep.

LETHARGY

Gathering all things hurrying up
before lethargy dilates the distance
between hand and door
—the den excavated with care in the paper:
straw provisions dry branches—
the lantern is lit up
that in the century was tempest and flame.

SOGNO (IN VERDE)

Come una grande Elisabetta nello scanno
la signora del verde con tutta la sua corte
stanotte ostruiva l'uscita senza malachite
di collane ramina di ciotole e albarelli
né onda di prato aroma di aranceti,
un adagio per muffe per licheni che era
ardenza di nero marcescenza di grandi
foglie tropicali deriva di ossido di rame
invalicabile cerchio di epatite.

QUELLA DELL'ISTANTE ALLENTATO

Quella dell'istante allentato del filo
che s'impiglia tra roghi di maestrale
—la strada intasata invasa di fumo
la galleria—quel giorno
in mezzo al bosco al crepitare
della ginestra sul barbecue
di grasso nero e cartine allo spiedo.

DREAM (IN GREEN)

Like great Elizabeth on her throne
the lady of greenery with all her court
last night obstructed the exit without malachite
of necklaces copper of bowls and birch bolete
neither meadow wave nor aroma of orange grove,
an adagio for mold and lichen that was
ardency of black rot of large
tropical leaves drift of copper oxide
impassable circle of hepatitis.

THAT OF THE SLACK INSTANT

That of the slack instant of thread
that gets entangled in bonfire of mistral
—the street clogged invaded by smoke
the gallery—that day
in the wood at the crackling
of the ginestra on the barbeque
of black fat and skewered cigarette paper.

CENA A DUE (TERRAZZA IN STILE ANDALUSO)
Il dio dei giorni uguali e dell'indifferenza
banchetta la sera tra i rampicanti
in bilico sulla pianura
di basi missilistiche di sciare
—occhi negli occhi mano nella mano—
tutto pronto per l'esecuzione:
testine in umido rosso d'annata.

PAESAGGIO
Un vizio di forma un verme
di lattuga s'insinuò nel paesaggio
ridefinito a secco senza magma.
Fiamma: l'attesi tutto il giorno.
Si presentò a mezzanotte: zolfo bagnato
bombardiere ronzante sulle case.

DINNER FOR TWO (ANDALUSIAN TERRACE)

The god of indistinct days and indifference

banquets in evening among the vines

tethered on the plain

of missile bases of lava ravines

—eyes into eyes hand in hand—

everything ready for the execution:

stewed calf's head red vintage.

SCENERY

A vice of form a lettuce worm

insinuated in the scenery

dried redefined without magma.

Flame: I waited for it the entire day.

It presented itself at midnight: wet sulphur

bomber buzzing over the houses.

LINGUA

Non so dove sei persa lingua
un tempo parlavi mille dialetti
ora balbetti inciampi
sibilante fax a vuoto nella stanza
segreto crepitare che di notte
senza segni di riconoscimento spinge
tra le atone dune, l'implacabile vento.

TONGUE

I do not know where you are lost tongue

once upon a time you spoke a thousand dialects

now you stutter and stumble

fax hissing in vain in the room

secret rustle that in the night

without signs of acknowledgment pushes

through atonal dunes, the implacable wind.

AMNESIA DEL
MOVIMENTO DELLE NUVOLE

———————

AMNESIA OF THE
MOVEMENT OF CLOUDS

Così nella foresta ove il mio spirito si rifugia,
un vecchio Ricordo suona a perdifiato il suo corno.
E penso ai marinai dimenticati su un' isola,
ai prigionieri, ai vinti … e molti altri ancora.

CHARLES BAUDELAIRE

———————

Thus in the forest where my soul takes refuge,
an ancient Memory sounds loud its hunting horn.
I think of the sailors forgotten on some isle, of the captives,
of the vanquished … and of many others too.

CHARLES BAUDELAIRE

IN FUGA, A BRANCHI

Risalimmo le lettere del libro
il mistero della luce a spirale
nella stanza—a branchi, in fuga,
non si sa da chi da quanto—ribaltando
il silenzio in algido fondo
astrale.

NEL MONDO DELLE EPOCHE

Nel mondo delle epoche echeggiavano risate
vibrazioni come tuoni tempeste in lontananza
erano invece i parlanti—guerre epidemie campi
minati e campi di sterminio—avremmo voluto
soffrire per quelli, portare un qualche aiuto
—Spartaco a Roma è crocefisso—eravamo
ciechi e resistenti: grumo afasico e incolore
che non volendo era.

IN FLIGHT, IN HERDS

We reclimbed the letters of the book
the mystery of the spiral light
in the stanza—in herds, in flight,
not knowing who from for how long—capsizing
silence in frigid astral depth.

IN THE WORLD OF EPOCHS

In the world of epochs echoed laughters
vibrations like thunder tempests in distance
were instead the speakers—wars epidemics mined
fields and killing fields—we would have liked
to suffer for them, bring some help
—Spartacus is crucified in Rome—we were
blind and obdurate: aphasic and colorless lump
that unwillingly was.

... ODIAVO L'INVERNO

... odiavo l'inverno e mi dispiacque
essere ameba nella notte antartica
—sorte di bianco in bianco acuminato
letargo—aspettando tra le tempeste
che Maggellano doppiasse Capo Horn
o che un qualche animale sulla tolda
mi metabolizzasse in balzo di tigre
nella savanna. Al buio continuai la mia corsa,
poi gli occhi vicinissimi allo specchio
verdi, radianti . . . .

FOSSILE A GIAVA

Fossile a Giava nel pleistocene e foglia
di menta nell'insalata di limone
che una bambina nel cinquanta
mangiava all'alba seduta al balcone
scivolando
tra glaciazione e glaciazione.

... I HATED WINTERS

... I hated winters and was sorry
to be amoeba in antartic night
—a kind of white in acute white
lethargy—waiting through the tempests
for Magellan to round Cape Horn
or for some animal on the awning
to metabolize me in a tiger's leap
in the savannah. In the dark I continued my run,
then the eyes very close to the mirror
green, radiant ....

FOSSIL IN JAVA

Fossil in Java in the pleistocene and leaf
of mint in the lemon salad
that a child in the 1950s
ate at dawn sitting on the balcony
sliding
between one glacial epoch and another.

SI INCONTRARONO ...

Si incontrarono alla corte del Re Sole
—lei, orchidea venuta dall'America,
lui, acuminato intelletto di Voltaire—finsero
di non conoscersi, o forse davvero
in quella vita non si riconobbero, nell'altra
magma di elettroni e minuetto.

UN RULLO DI TAMBURI ...

Un rullo di tamburi l'ha svegliato
dalle buie cavità del Settecento
Cagliostro col suo corteo di figuranti
—saltibanchi poeti giocolieri i giullari
dell'alto Medioevo col campanello
della pazzia—accende il porfido
nello scantinato del secolo che muore
l'oro sepolto la barca capovolta
per traghettare, insieme, la notte
ricomporre
l'incoerente brusio in bianca conoscenza.

THEY MET ...

They met at the court of Louis the Great
—she, an orchid from America,
he, sharp intellect of Voltaire—pretended
they did not recognize each other, or maybe in truth
they did not in that life, in the other
magma of electrons and minuets.

A ROLL OF DRUMS ...

A roll of drums awoke him
from the dark cavities of the eighteenth century
Cagliostro with his throng of characters
—acrobats poets jugglers the fools
of the early Middle Ages—he ignites the porphyry
in the basement of the century that dies
the gold buried the ship turned upside down
to ferry, together, the night
recomposing
the incoherent bristle in white knowledge.

LA SEDIA CHE LA SUA MANO ...

La sedia che la sua mano impagliò

e disperse le sue tracce

tra il bianco delle infermerie e il freddo

dei notomizzati nel buio lessicale

che fu

schianto di temporale tra gli agrumeti

estate di fumo nei campi del quaranta.

Arbeit macht frei.

THE CHAIR THAT HIS HAND ...

The chair that his hand stuffed

and scattered its traces

in white of infimaries and cold

of those dissected in lexical darkness

that was

crash of storm in orange groves

summer of smoke in the fields of 1940s.

Arbeit macht frei.

... di colpo la parola *smarrimento* subito dopo l'altra

seicento—facili rime assonanze mi dicevo nel sonno—

affondando tra i liquami nel lazzaretto di Palermo

dove fui medico alla Gran Corte—di nome Ingrassia—

con infusi alchimie salvavo dalla morte gli appestati,

l'anno dopo da ignota mano avvelenato a corte per invidia ....

..... morivo

a poco a poco risalendo tra le strade di Parigi sul finire

del secolo dei lumi *Viva Saint Just! Viva Robespierre!*

Fu sentenza di morte. Sula carretta verso la ghigliottina

domandai chi fossi al Capitano Giustiziere indicó

nel folto di una schiera un ragazzo imbottito di tritolo

in Palestina, e un'altra, lapidata ...

.... nel frattempo, ero già morta ....

Era la notte del diciannove giugno del 2002: non sapevo chi,

in quale modo ero.

... S U D D E N L Y   T H E   W O R D   *D I S O R I E N T A T I O N* ...

.... suddenly the word *disorientation* immediately after the other

six-hundred—easy rhymes assonances I muttered to myself in my sleep—

plunging in the slurry of Palermo's lazaret

where I was a doctor at the great court—named Ingrassia—

with alchemy infusion I saved the lives of the infected

the following year by unknown hand poisoned at the court out of envy ....

..... I died

little by little ascending the streets of Paris near the end

of the enlightement *Viva Saint Just! Viva Robespierre!*

It was a death sentence. On the cart on the way to the guillottine

I asked who I was to the Chief Executioner he pointed out

in the thick of a crowd a boy stuffed with TNT

in Palestine, and another girl, stoned to death ...

.......in the meantime, I was already dead ....

It was the night of the nineteenth of June of 2002: I did not know
who, in what manner I was.

SQUAME OCCHI A FESSURA ...

Squame occhi a fessura quella volta
movimento ondulatorio della testa
che nascosi tra calle e pesci nella vasca
giugno a colpi d'accetta e pietrate biscia
a pezzi davanti alla porta.

DAPPRIMA LABILI SEGNI ...

Dapprima labili segni di creature di passo
impercettibili voli di uccelli acquatici
cicogne coturnici—poi desquamazioni
stagionali tra gli interstizi depositi di nero
di un'ignota fauna stanziale—incroci
di ratti e millepiedi virus giganti
scorpioni malformati—l'embolo pazzo
tra le coperte, negli armadi il vento.

SCALES SLIT-EYES ...

Scales slit-eyes that time
ondulating movement of the head
that I hid among the calla lillies and the fish in the pool
June with hatchet blows and stones grass snake
in pieces at the doorstep.

AT FIRST FAINT SIGNS ...

At first faint signs of passing creatures
imperceptible flight of water birds
yellow-billed storks—then seasonal
desquamation between crevices droppings of black
of unknown resident fauna—hybrids
of rats and centipedes gigantic viruses
deformed scorpions—the mad embolus
between the blankets, wind in the closets.

ERA MIA ...

Era mia, nell'incorrotto sfero di Parmenide,
l'onda di fiume la mano anonima che in sogno
ti accarezza: oscura simmetria di fuoco e acqua
inconsapevole frusciare di neuroni.
Fu discordia
il verminoso brulicare in carne di albicocca, divisi
nella notte cosmogonia da un profondo scorrere
di particelle scambi da un buio cercarsi di elettroni
fino alla sintesi, qui, tra mercanti e affamati,
scarafaggio di Kafka coscienza che muore.

OGNI TENTACOLO UN OCCHIO ...

Ogni tentacolo un occhio
ogni squama una zampa
presente di calcinacci di nuvole in transito
senza destinatario oltre le basse colline la piana
di melograni e ossidiana dove s'accampano
i rifugiati in una finzione di stasi
drago serpente
tra il respiro e la bocca.

Amnesia del movimiento delle nuvole
buio di encefalo spento.

IT WAS MINE ...

It was mine, in the uncorrupted sphere of Parmenides
the river wave the anonymous hand that in the dream
strokes you: dark symmetry of fire and water
unconscious rustle of neurons.
It was disagreement
the swarmy overflowing in apricot flesh, divided
in the cosmogony of night from the deep flow
of particles exchanges from the blind seeking of electrons
to the synthesis, here, among the merchants and the hungry,
Kafka's beetle consciousness that dies.

EACH TENTACLE AN EYE ...

Each tentacle an eye
each scale a paw
present time of rubble of transit of clouds
without addressee beyond the low hills the plain
of pomegranate trees and obsidian where refugees
camp in a fiction of stasis
dragon snake
between breath and mouth.

Amnesia of the movement of clouds
darkness of spent encephalus.

UN TRANSITO DI NUVOLE ...

Un transito di nuvole sul mare gorghi ombre filamenti
biancore progressivo galleggiando
fino ai dettagli nitidi di un improvviso mattino
—venditori d'acqua sulla spiaggia cicogne vigili sulle rovine—
tra un brusio di ignoti transiti di storia che si fa
in un martedì di esplosioni ad occidente

                                        auscultando

il rullare d'acqua e vento nell'oceano battuto dal maestrale
—scafisti in fuga squali sulle fiancate—il gorgo d'amnesia
che da un'atlantica città di palme e ciminiere
risale gli stretti i meridiani forza le porte dell'isola blindata
debordando tra i bunker dell'entroterra
si frange in fossili sui parapetti cancella gli atti documentali

                                        lo schianto

dall'altra perte del mare che replica l'ibiscus
le ciminiere i giochi dei ragazzi sulla spiaggia
declinante sequenza il passo clandestino il gemito
di Eschilo che muore senza giustizia
tra le colonne del promontorio
torme di popoli nell'acqua

                                nube di Oort alla deriva.

A TRANSIT OF CLOUDS ...
    A transit of clouds on the sea whirlpools shadows filaments
    increasing whiteness floating
    up to the sharp details of a sudden morning
    —water bottles vendors on the beach vigilant storks on the ruins—
    in a murmur of unknowns transit of history that is made
    in a Tuesday of explosions in the West

                                     harkening

the rolling of water and wind in the ocean whipped by mistral
—smugglers in flight sharks at the flanks—the whirlpool of amnesia
that from an Atlantic city of palms and smokestacks
reclimbs the straits the meridians forces the doors of the armored island
overflowing from hinterland bunkers
breaks into fossils on the railings erases documented papers

                                     the crash

from the other side of the ocean that replicates the hibiscus
the smokestacks the boys' games on the beach
declining sequence the clandestine step the moan
of Aeschylus who dies without justice
between the columns of the promontory
throngs of people in the water

                                 Oort cloud adrift.

SENTIVO OGNI GIORNO ...

Sentivo ogni giorno un indice destro
digitarmi ma non riuscii a decifrare
il tocco a spirale che accese
la dialettica dell'onda e del veliero
le ombre degli alberi contro il cielo di notte.
Fu sete guerra nucleo radioattivo
passando come un rumore d'acqua persa
tra gli strati di buio e di chiarore
la forma oscura che mi dorme accanto
—ferita mai riscattata dalla storia. Un virus
risalì i circuiti cancellò la schermata.

UN ATTIMO UNO SOLO ...

Un attimo uno solo—assoluto
in cima al campanile—luce
di sofferenza intelligente
che tace nell'occhio del mattino
senza scissure fraintendimenti
si guarda e non si riconosce,
il dio imperfetto, la grande amnesia.

I FELT EACH DAY ...

I felt each day an index of the right hand

digitize me but I could not decipher

the spiral touch that turned on

the dialectic of wave and mast

the shadows of the trees against the night sky.

It was silk war radioactive nucleus

passing by like a noise of water lost

between the layers of darkness and glimmering

the obscure from that sleeps next to me

—wound never redeemed by history. A virus

reclimbed the circuits erased the screen.

A MOMENT ONLY ONE ...

A moment only one—absolute

atop the belltower—light

of intelligent suffering

silent in the eye of morning

without divisions misunderstandings

looks at and doesn't recognize itself,

the imperfect god, the great amnesia.

DEL ROSSO E NERO VERSO

———————

OF RED AND BLACK VERSE

(La notte abbassa le saracinesche
mostra gli artigli le zampe
aprendo un labirinto
in mezzo al pavimento in bilico
tra stasi e movimento il rosso
ha l'apparenza del rosso
la vita della vita)

(Night lowers the gates
shows its claws the paws
opening a labyrinth
in the middle of the floor unstable
between stasis and movement the red
appears as red
life as life)

I

Il bianco dilagò nella scrittura
come un fiume di latte un giro di candeggio
—*cliccare cosa?* chiesi
alla città turrita alla porta sbarrata—
persa nella cieca videata
tra files occultati arti senza connessioni.

II

Nella campagna a cotone e tabacco
del cinquanta risuonò
lo zoccolo di mulo di una scrittura
disobbediente la lumaca perse
il suo tracciato la gazza fu serpente
tra i segni della grammatica sconnessa
rigurgiti d'acqua affondamenti
—gebbia lippusa
dove vacilla il piede a sette anni.

I

White flooded the writing
like a river of milk a cycle of bleach
—*clicking what?* I asked
the towered city the barred door—
lost in the blind screen
among hidden files limbs without connections.

II

In the countryside of cotton and tobacco
of the 1950s resounded
the mule hoof of a disobedient
writing the snail lost
its trace the magpie became snake
among the signs of disconnected grammar
regurgitations of water sinkings
—mossy cistern
where the foot vacillates at seven years old.

III (COMPLEANNO)

Come un'anima in pena un osso di albicocca
in vuota fruttiera tra sacchi di immondizia
detriti della discarica in cerca di che non sapeva.
Travestita da prete entrò in una chiesa
e disse messa: i santi nelle nicchie
la guardarono incazzati. Gridò scivolò
resistette spinta infine sul carro merci
tra i rastrellati. Suonavano le sette
all'orologio della stazione—il due febbraio
del quarantatré—fra sibili e nomi alla ruota.

IV (FALLUJA)

A crepe a lingue appese ai ganci
cercando il varco
il passaggio per riversarci intatti
—sul ponte un passo dopo l'altro—
nel fiume tra resti d'imballaggio
una bambina disidratata
sciolta dal fosforo bianco.

III (BIRTHDAY)

As a soul in pain the pit of an apricot
in empty fruit bowl among trash bags
landfill rubble looking not knowing for what.
Disguised as a priest she entered a church
and celebrated mass: saints in their niches
looked on infuriated. She screamed fell
resisted was pushed finally on the freight train
with the rounded-up. Seven o'clock
chimed in the station—February second
1943 —among hisses and names at the wheel.

IV (FALLUJA)

In crevices in tongues hung to hooks
searching for the breach
the passage to pour ourselves whole
—on the bridge one step after another—
in the river with the dregs of packing
a girl dehydrated
melted by white phosphorus.

V (ACUFENI: PER MIA MADRE)

Giallo di canarino soccorri la barrata

tra mulini e ingranaggi—le sequenze

del retablo impallidite l'iride verde

appannata—la dissonanza accende

il vuoto di memoria il martello infuocato

—orto concluso dove muore il tempo—

seduta accanto alla finestra

stringe i braccioli cerca la figlia

in fuga nella città che si risveglia

guardando il volo dell'ultimo nato in gabbia.

VI

A cenni a sordità

dall'altra parte del crepaccio

gridando "eccomi

sono qua" immobile

sul ciglio della notte

alla chiamata.

V (TINNITUS: FOR MY MOTHER)
    Canary yellow you assist the barred hen

    amid the mills and gears—sequences

    of retablo paled green iris

    dimmed—dissonance sparks

    the void of memory scalding hammer

    —closed orchard where time dies—

    seated beside the window

    she clutches the armrests searches for a daughter

    who flees through the city waking

    looking at the flight of the last born in the cage.

VI
    By gestures in deafness

    from the other side of the chasm

    shouting "it's me

    I am here" unmoved

    on the verge of the night

    by the call.

VII

S'insinuò nel tubo catodido e spense
i candelabra della fortuna emocromo
distratto tra caso e necessità
risalendo
fino alla cavità dell'avanbraccio.
Chiama per nome. Dice: "*Basta!*"

VIII

Goccia e foglia
oscuro nodo di carena
che all'improvviso si spezzò
riaffondando. Scienza
di spigolosi nomi,
tipo: sorte-morte.

VII

Insinuated in the cathode ray tube and switched off
the chandeliers of fortune haemochrome
distracted between fate and necessity
reclimbing
to the cavity of the forearm.
Calls by name. Says: "*Enough!*"

VIII

Drop and leaf
obscure knot of keel
that suddenly snapped
again sinking. Science
of angular names,
type: toss-loss.

I X

Il nome prese forma di merlo
nel paesaggio invernale arrivarono
altri animali in bianco e nero la gazza
il randagio pezzato mio padre
—fascista ostinato morto da quarant'anni—
con la maschera antigas in Abissinia
"muoiono come topi intrappolati"
dice e si compiace scalando
in divisa da soldato il secolo
di nebbia e case dirupate
(il nome in forma di osso di seppia
di bomba a grappolo nella spianata).

IX

The name took on the form of a blackbird
in wintry landscape arrived
other animals in black and white a magpie
a motley stray my father
—fascist obstinate dead for forty years—
with gas mask in Abyssinia
"they die like trapped mice"
he says and congratulates with himself ascending
in soldier uniform the century
of fog and destroyed houses
(the name in the form of a cuttlefish bone
of a cluster bomb in the clearing).

X (LETTERA A UN AMANTE MORTO)

Amore mio—pagina scritta anemico testo di poesia—
ci provo a dirti come stanno le cose. Che stanno malissimo.
Nostro figlio a dieci anni ricoverato nel reparto incurabili,
e l'amico tuo—il filosofo del pensiero forte—
promuove filosofie in televendita.
Una scrittura disobbediente devia fiumi e petroliere
scavando crepe tra gli zigomi e il mento
omologando ai mercati la torre di Babele.
E umani rottamati a fini produttivi.
Ogni tanto di notte sento un fiotto di grida che proviene dal mare
—un clandestino mi dico sta annegando—
tappo finestre e tivù mi chiudo ermetica tra i segni
aspettando che si faccia giorno, ma sogno martelli
coltelli da cucina punteruoli in questa veglia sbieca di morenti.
Un'ultima cosa, risibile se vuoi,
i negative delle foto li ho persi nel trasloco,
e non li ho più trovati intelletto e verità.
Esposte a scarpe chiodate al gelo dei mattoni
le nostre figure di passione.

X (LETTER TO A DEAD LOVER)
My love—page of writing anemic text of poetry—
I'll try to tell you how things are. They're really bad.
Our son at ten hospitalized in the terminal ward,
and your friend—the philosopher of strong thought—
promotes philosophies with telemarketing.
A disobedient writing makes rivers and tankers deviate
digging crevices between chin and cheekbones
approving the tower of Babel for the market.
And people scrapped for productive ends.
Sometimes at night I hear a gush of screams coming from the sea
—a clandestine I tell myself is drowning—
I seal windows and TV I shut myself hermetic among signs
waiting for daylight, but dream of hammers
kitchen knives awls in this slanted wake of dying people.
A last thing, laughable if you will,
the negatives of the photos I lost them in the move,
and never found them again intellect and truth.
Exposed to studded boots and the cold of bricks
our figures of passion.

XI

Tutta apparata di incenso e orecchini
ripeteva a mente le filastrocche
i nomi segnati su mappe infantili
ma lei—anima bella—
con tutte le giunture e i fili in ordine
tardava gorgheggiando
finte sequenze di corsi e di ricorsi.
Esaurita la lotta di classe dismise
orecchini e buone maniere splendeva
un rosso di genocidi tra saccheggi
e occupanti prese il fucile la mira ....

XII (M A N - D - O R L O)

Dalla cima alle radici
dell'albero dei nomi: il mandorlo
si spezzò in *man* e *orlo*—orlo di vita
scucito e ricucito ogni mattina—
la *d* balbettando volò via.
Taci, trattieni il respire, sorellina,
l'ora delle parole dormienti
si fa vicina, vicina.

XI

All decked in incense and earrings
she recited the nursery rhymes by heart
the names marked on childish maps
but she—beautiful soul—
with all her joints and threads in order
lingered warbling
false sequences of courses and recourses.
Exhausted the class war she dismissed
the earrings and her good manners a red
of genocides was shining between pillaging
and occupying troops she took the gun and aimed ...

XII (MAN-D-ORLO)

Form the tip to the roots
of the tree of names: the almond
snapped in *man* and *orlo*—orlo of life
unraveled and sewn back together every morning—
the *d* stammering flew away.
Hush, hold your breath, little sister,
the hour of sleeping words
is getting near, near.

XIII

L'iride si aprì
sulla maniglia della porta
cercando
nelle isole di muffa sul muro
nella carta d'imballaggio in cucina
"dove sei" disse, e non trovando
si rinchiuse tra resti di caffè
alberi indifferenti al testo.

XIV

… mentre il belare mentre l'acqua e la mente mentre il
ruotare del secolo si ferma davanti alla porta non distillare,
attimo, i tuoi acidi, un rasoterra di vita svampa in luce di
parola nella stanza un limpido giorno a novembre
precipitando nell'ora …

XIII

The iris opened
on the doorknob
searching
in islands of mildew on the wall
in the wrapping paper in the kitchen
"where are you" it said, and not finding
shut itself up amid in the coffee dregs
trees indifferent to the text.

XIV

… while the bleating while the water and the mind while the
turning of the century stops in front of the door do not distill,
moment, your acids, a grazing of life dies out under the light of
words in the room a limpid day in November
precipitating in the hour …

(Rime nere—insincere—
aprirono le porte ai condannati
alle fuggenti frotte. La terapia
fu d'urto, la pagina si svuotò
e si svuotò del nero anche la stanza.
Ultima ratio: l'odore delle fresie
il mio vestito rosso.)

(Black rhymes—insincere—
opened the doors to the condemned
the fleeing throng. Shock
therapy, the page emptied
and emptied also of black was the stanza.
Last ratio: the smell of freesia
my red dress.)

TRANSLATOR'S NOTES

The Italian edition of *Amnesia of the Movements of Clouds* presents, in appendix, a few notes prepared by Maria Attanasio. Three of these notes explain the Sicilian terms *alluciata* and *allupata* and the Sicilian expression *morte buttana*. The remaining notes provide historical commentary or contextualize the writing of individual poems. Attanasio's explanations are incorporated here and enlarged upon, with additional notes added for the English-language reader.

UNA FRAZIONE DI NON COINCIDENZA /
A FRACTION OF NONCOINCIDENCE

> la cittá sull'altura / *the city on high ground*: Caltagirone, Attanasio's city of birth and residence. Built on a mountain rising 610 meters above sea level (2,000 feet), Caltagirone appears from a distance as a compact and self-contained city, blending into its geological substratum.

UN FULMINE UNA GRANDE CASCATA /
A FLASH OF LIGHTNING A GREAT CASCADE

> zolfanello / *match*: A sulphur-tipped match, or a wick imbued with sulphur, used to light up oil lamps. In Sicily, where sulphur is mined in the south-west area near Agrigento, the term *zolfanello* is used instead of the standard Italian *fiammifero* to indicate a sulphur match. This regional use is an example of Attanasio's *lingua lippusa* (see translator's introduction).

UN PIEDE AVANTI POI L'ALTRO /
ONE FOOT FORWARD THEN THE OTHER

> monatto: In the Middle Ages, a *monatto* was an undertaker: a lowly laborer paid monthly to handle corpses and other unpleasant duties. In the sixteenth and seventeenth centuries, during the many waves of plague, this term acquired the special meaning of a city employee hired to collect corpses, burn their

possessions, clean their homes, and bury them. Other duties included the deportation of those who had contracted plague to militarized hospital camps where all carriers were confined and kept in complete isolation from their families, often against their will. The public perception of the *monatti* was unfavorable. As Alessandro Manzoni shows in his historical novel about the 1630 plague in Milan, *The Betrothed*, the *monatti* were seen as preying on the dead, stealing their possessions, and abusing their families. No English translation exists for this term.

PARLARE DELLA MORTE POI SCOPARE / *TO TALK ABOUT DEATH AND THEN TO FUCK*

In her notes to the Italian edition of *Amnesia*, Attansio dedicates this poem to the late poet and novelist Salvatore Addamo, her "teacher in life and writing." She adds: "if he could have read this poem … he certainly would have objected: for the too-explicit sentiment."

DELLA FORZATA RIMA / *OF FORCED RHYME*

Louis Soliano's epigraph marking this section of *Amnesia* is Attanasio's own writing: the author, Soliano, is her invention, although, as Attanasio notes, "he could have existed in a Borgesian labyrinth."

INCIPIT (UN NOME A CASO) / *INCIPIT (A NAME BY CHANCE)*

Lisa lisetta lisavetta: A compact cascade of meaning descends from the opening word of this poem, reflecting Attanasio's attention to the "rising cultural stratification of words" (as she puts it in an unpublished note). *Lisa* is of course a woman's name, but also the singular, feminine form of an adjective meaning worn-out, threadbare, consumed. The two words that follow develop meanings prompted by that adjective and would, if upper case, be diminutives of the name. Since an Italian reader would find the suggestion of those diminutives inescapable and since the sonic linkage of these three words is primary, I left them untranslated. As a modified form of the adjective *lisa*, *lisetta* keeps the original meaning of being worn out, thread-bare, and consumed, but also indicates that these qualifications apply to a young or a petite woman. The modified form of the adjective is also a slight term of endearment (in Italian, a *vezzeggiativo*) that marks a turn to pathos, affect. The third term, *lisavetta*, literally means a worn-out, old, shorn mountain peak (*vetta* is "peak"). As a proper name, Lisavetta has two important literary references: it is the name of the innocent maid killed by the aristocratic hero Raskolnikov in Fyodor Dostoyevsky's *Crime and Punishment* and the name of the independent woman artist in Thomas Mann's *Tonio Kröger*. *Lisavetta*, therefore, if taken as a diminutive of *Lisa*, is a term of endearment permeated with pity, with the literary allusions conveying the sense of being worn out, consumed by work, social injustice, alienation, and poverty.

INCIPIT (UN NOME A CASO) /
INCIPIT (A NAME BY CHANCE)

atro ostello ... atra sorte / *dark hostel ... bitter fate*: A deepening in the layering of the sense of alienation suggested by the poem is revealed if the archaic Italian words *atro* and *atra* are read with an ear attuned to Sicilian pronunciation, so that they become *autro* and *autra*—the masculine and feminine forms of the Sicilian adverb for "other." If read as *Autro ostello ... autra sorte*, lines three and five of the poem would thus acquire the new meaning "other hostel ... other fate."

ALIMENTARISTA / NUTRITIONIST

alluciata / *blinded*: As Attanasio explains in the notes that accompany the Italian edition of *Amnesia*, *alluciata* (and the corresponding verb, *alluciare*) is used in Sicilian with the meaning of being blinded by an intense stream of light, or even, Attanasio writes, being "annihilated" by the force of light. The term, however, is not exclusively Sicilian but descends from the archaic Italian verb *alluciare* and carries the meaning of "staring intensely." This verb has fallen into disuse in contemporary Italian, where *abbacinare* (to dazzle) is used instead.

Both meanings, old and new, Italian and Sicilian, are present in this example of Attanasio's *lingua lippusa*, but in this case, as Attanasio indicates, the Sicilian meaning is more important. (I should note here that *alluciare* also still exists in the Tuscan dialect as spoken in Lucca, where it now means "glancing.")

REPENTE / *SUDDENLY*

allupata / *ravenous*: An archaic adjective, commonly used in Sicilian, that indicates both being hungry and being stealthy as a wolf (*lupo*, wolf, is in the radix of this word). The term also has the connotations of being predatory and capable of suddenly appearing or disappearing. As Attanasio notes in the Italian edition of *Amnesia*, the term *allupato* is a reminder of a not-so-distant past when wolves would emerge from the forest and threaten men and animals, disappearing just as quickly when confronted.

FUSIONE / *FUSION*

suono a lutto / *mourning sound*: A reinforcement of the meaning is revealed if these words are read with an ear attuned to Sicilian pronunciation, with *suono a lutto* sliding into the similar-sounding *sono a lutto*, (I am in mourning, I am grieving).

LACCATA DI ROSSO / *VARNISHED IN RED*

moussem: Annual fair in Morocco, a festive celebration of cultural and religious traditions.

MORTE BUTTANA / *DEATH BITCH*

Title: A very common Sicilian expression indicating a state of great anger at a sudden and unpleasant event.

PASSATO (IN ERI) / *PAST (YOU WERE)*

Steri: The idiomatic name of Chiaramonte Palace in Palermo, Sicily. Built on the eve of the fourteenth century, the palace was the residence of kings and viceroys, and the seat of the Tribunal of Inquisition for many centuries. *Steri* comes from *hosterium*, fortified palace. *Steri* is also a measure, the equivalent of "cord."   ,

NOTIZIA DI CRONACA (11 GENNAIO '99) / LOCAL NEWS (11 JANUARY 1999)

Title: As widely reported in the press, members of the United Self-Defense Forces of Colombia (AUC), Colombia's largest paramilitary organization, raided the villages of six districts of southern Columbia on the ninth of January,1999, torturing and executing more than 150 villagers, women and children included, in retaliation for a FARC attack on the AUC headquarters at El Nudo de Paramillo in December. Attanasio dates the execution erroneously, perhaps marking the day in which she completed writing the poem.

LUDICA MENTE / PLAYFUL MIND

Title: This could be heard as one word, *ludicamente*, that is, "playfully."

(FORZATA) RIMA IN ÌA / (FORCED) IA RHYME

storìa / *historia*: With the accent on the *i*, Attanasio elegantly introduces the Sicilian pronunciation of the Italian *storia* (history). I adopt *historia* to convey the intended sound, so crucial to this poem.

QUELLA DELL'ISTANTE ALLENTATO / THAT OF THE SLACK INSTANT

ginestra: Spanish broom (*spartium junceum*), a fragrant plant very common in Sicily and in the southern regions of Europe.

UN RULLO DI TAMBURI ... / A ROLL OF DRUMS ...

In her notes, Attanasio explains that this poem is dedicated to the "artist, patron of the arts, and elective brother" Antonio Presti (Cagliostro in the poem). The note also narrates the contextual and intertextual references contained in the poem. She writes (the bracketed insertions are mine):

> [Antonio Presti] loves to say that "Beauty shines brighter in the heart of those who desire it than in the eyes of those who see it"; in the name of beauty, inviolable right, and utopia, in March 2001 he designed and realized *The Poets' Train*, and, earlier, from the mid-1980s until the late 1990s, *The Stream of Art*, an installation of sculpture and poetry disseminated along the dry streambeds between Tusa and Pettineo [two villages in the northwest of Sicily, near Messina]. This poem makes reference to the [art installation] of Nobuho Nagasawa *The Room of the Golden Boat*: a subterranean room underneath the Romei, a brook, with the installation of the Japanese artist inside the room—porphyry, gold, and an overturned boat—sealed in front of a notary and a crowd of artists. The boat will be reopened after one hundred years: in another, perhaps more just, epoch.

... DI COLPO LA PAROLA SMARRIMENTO /
... SUDDENLY THE WORD DISORIENTMENT

Ingrassia: As Attanasio points out in a note, Ingrassia, a court doctor in Palermo, was born in Caltagirone and was, in the seventeenth century, a highly regarded scholar, researcher, and an "extraordinary therapist of the plague." He "exerted a vast influence on the viceroy and was poisoned out of envy by unknown courtesans."

UN TRANSITO DI NUVOLE / A TRANSIT OF CLOUDS

Attanasio narrates the circumstances leading to the writing of this poem in the following note (the bracketed insertions are mine):

> I spent the summer of 2001 and many other summers between [the Moroccan city of] Mohammedia on the Atlantic coast and [the Sicilian city of] Gela on the Sicilian channel. These two places are dear to me and I think of them as sister cities: the same maritime tonalities, same

vegetation, the same smokestacks in the horizon [for Gela is a refinery of petrol piped in from Algeria], and the same history of globalization threatening them. I was in Mohammedia when I heard the news of the attack against the twin towers in New York on September 11, 2001, and this news blended with the obsessive image of my friend, the poet Salvo Basso, mortally ill, to whose memory *Amnesia* is dedicated.

NELLA CAMPAGNA A COTONE E TABACCO /
IN THE COUNTRYSIDE OF COTTON AND TOBACCO

lippusa / *mossy*: See translator's introduction for a discussion of this evocative Sicilian term.

TUTTA APPARATA DI INCENSE E ORECCHINI /
ALL DECKED IN INCENSE AND EARRINGS

apparata / *decked in*: Sicilian term, indicating a gaudy and theatrically excessive use of jewelry or decorative items of clothing.

(MAN-D-ORLO) / *(MAN-D-ORLO)*

Title: Attanasio breaks the word *mandorlo* (almond tree) into three words: *man* (abbreviated form of *mano*, hand), *d* (truncated form of *di*, of) and *orlo* (hem). *Man-d-orlo* thus reads "hand of the hem," vernacular Italian for "make a hem" (the entire expression in spoken language goes: *fare una mano d'orlo*).

MARIA ATTANASIO

Born in 1943 in Caltagirone, Italy, where she still lives and writes today, Maria Attanasio is the author of seven books of poetry, four of historical fiction (three novels and a collection of short stories), two of utopian fiction, and two of literary and social criticism, with a number of other texts in various genres yet to be collected. One of her latest works, *Il falsario di Caltagirone (The Counterfeiter of Caltagirone)* (Palermo: Sellerio 2007), has been the recipient of the prestigious Premio Vittorini. Her books of poetry are *Interni (Interiors)* (Milano: Guanda 1979), *Nero barocco nero (Black Baroque Black)* (Caltanissetta: Sciascia 1985), *Eros e mente (Eros and Mind)* (Milano: La Vita Felice 1996), *Ludica mente (Ludic Mind, or Ludically)* (Roma: Avagliano 2000), *Amnesia del movimento delle nuvole (Amnesia of the Movement of Clouds)* (Milano: La Vita Felice 2003), *Frammenti dell'acqua mutante (Fragments of the Mutable Water)* (Roma: Signum edizioni d'arte 2010), and *Del rosso e nero verso (Of Red and Black Verse)* (Milano: Il Faggio 2007). Her works in prose include *Correva l'anno 1698 e nella citta' avvenne il fatto memorabile (It Was the Year 1698 and in the City the Memorable Fact Occurred)* (Palermo: Sellerio 1994), *Di Concetta e le sue donne (Of Concetta and Her Women)* (Palermo: Sellerio 1999), *Della città di argilla (Of the City of Clay)* (Messina: Mesogea 2012), and *Il condominio di Via della Notte (The Condominium on Night Street)* (Palermo: Sellerio 2013). *Amnesia of the Movement of Clouds / Of Red and Black Verse* is the first full-length publication in English of Attanasio's work.

CARLA BILLITTERI

Carla Billitteri is the author of the critical study, *Language and the Renewal of Society in Walt Whitman, Laura (Riding) Jackson and Charles Olson* (Palgrave, 2009) and of numerous essays on English- and Italian-language poetry that have appeared in *Aerial, Arizona Quarterly, Gravesiana, How2, The Journal of Modern Literature, Paideuma, Textual Practice,* and *The Worcester Review.* She is also active as a translator of contemporary Italian poetry, with work in *The FSG Book of Twentieth-Century Italian Poetry, Aufgabe, Boundary2, How2, Fascicle,* and the *Atlanta Review.* An edition of her translations from Alda Merini's aphorisms was published by Hooke Press in 2008. She teaches poetry, poetics, and critical theory at the University of Maine at Orono where she is also a member of the editorial collective of The National Poetry Foundation.

LITMUS PRESS TITLES

Murder, Danielle Collobert, $18
    translated by Nathanaël
Then Go On, Mary Burger, $15
O Bon, Brandon Shimoda, $15
I Want to Make You Safe, Amy King, $15
How Phenomena Appear to Unfold, Leslie Scalapino, $24
Beauport, Kate Colby, $15
Time of Sky & Castles in the Air, Ayane Kawata, $18
    translated by Sawako Nakayasu
Portrait of Colon Dash Parenthesis, Jeffrey Jullich, $15
Hyperglossia, Stacy Szymaszek, $15
From Dame Quickly, Jennifer Scappettone, $15
Face Before Against, Isabelle Garron, $15
    translated by Sarah Riggs
Animate, Inanimate Aims, Brenda Iijima $15
Fruitlands, Kate Colby, $12
Counter Daemons, Roberto Harrison, $15
Emptied of All Ships, Stacy Szymaszek, $12
Inner China, Eva Sjödin, $12
    translated by Jennifer Hayashida
The Mudra, Kerri Sonnenberg, $12
Another Kind of Tenderness, Xue Di, $15
    translated by Keith Waldrop, Forrest Gander, Stephen Thomas,
    Theodore Deppe, and Sue Ellen Thompson
Euclid Shudders, Mark Tardi, $12
Notebooks: 1956–1978, Danielle Collobert, $12
    translated by Norma Cole
The House Seen from Nowhere, Keith Waldrop, $12

Venn Diagram Productions, published in collaboration with Belladonna Books:

NO GENDER: Reflections on the Life & Work of kari edwards
    edited by Julian T. Brolaski, erica kaufman, and E. Tracy Grinnell, $18
Bharat jiva, kari edwards, $15
Four From Japan: Contemporary Poetry & Essays by Women
    translated and with an introduction by Sawako Nakayasu, $14

green press
INITIATIVE

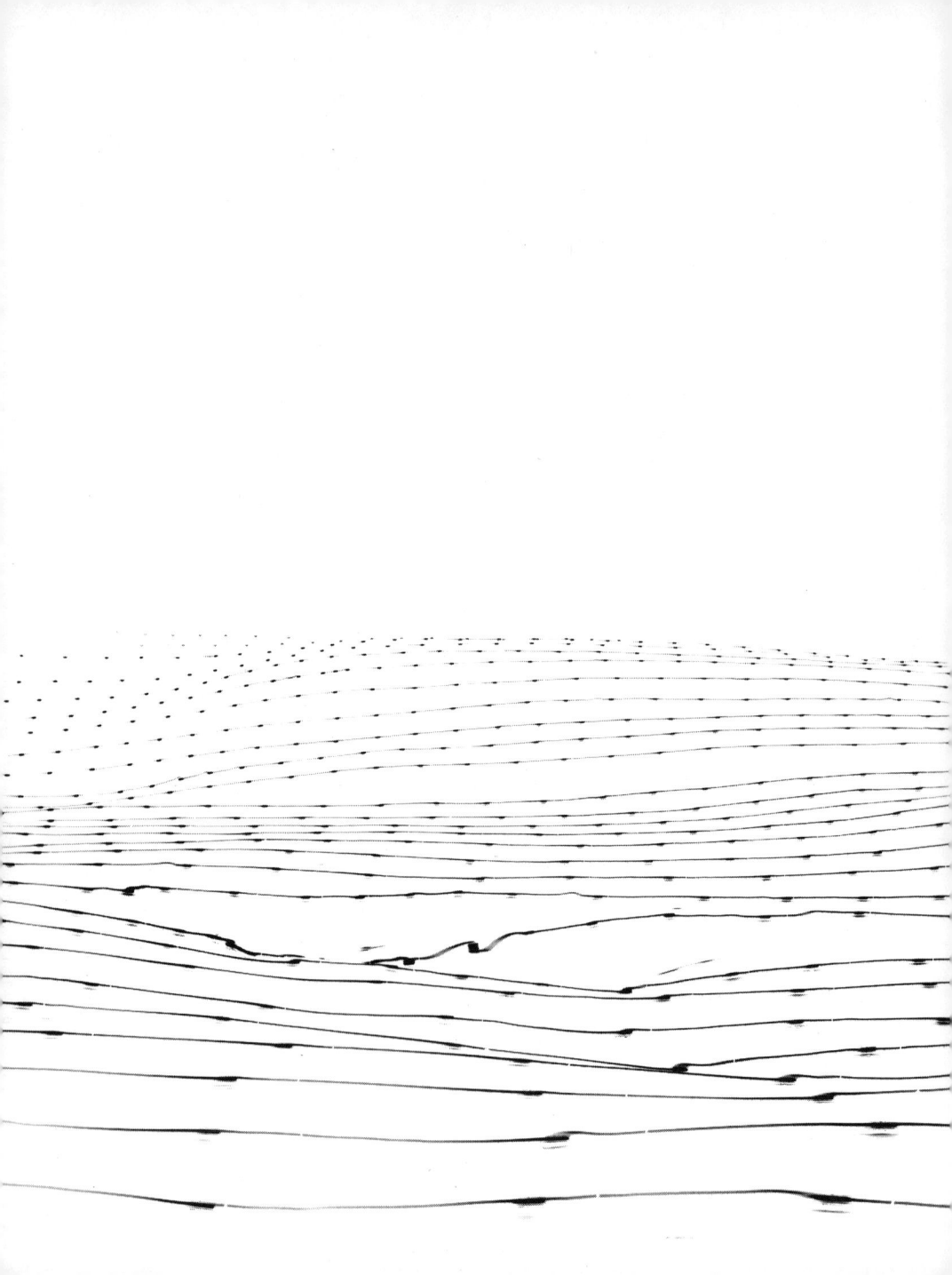